Piddle and Sniff
The everyday life of a magnificent pup

Dante Miles
As told to Edyth Miles

Illustrated by Hattie Hyder

Text Copyright © 2017 Edyth Miles
Illustrations © 2017 Hattie Hyder

All rights reserved.

ISBN:9781973201090

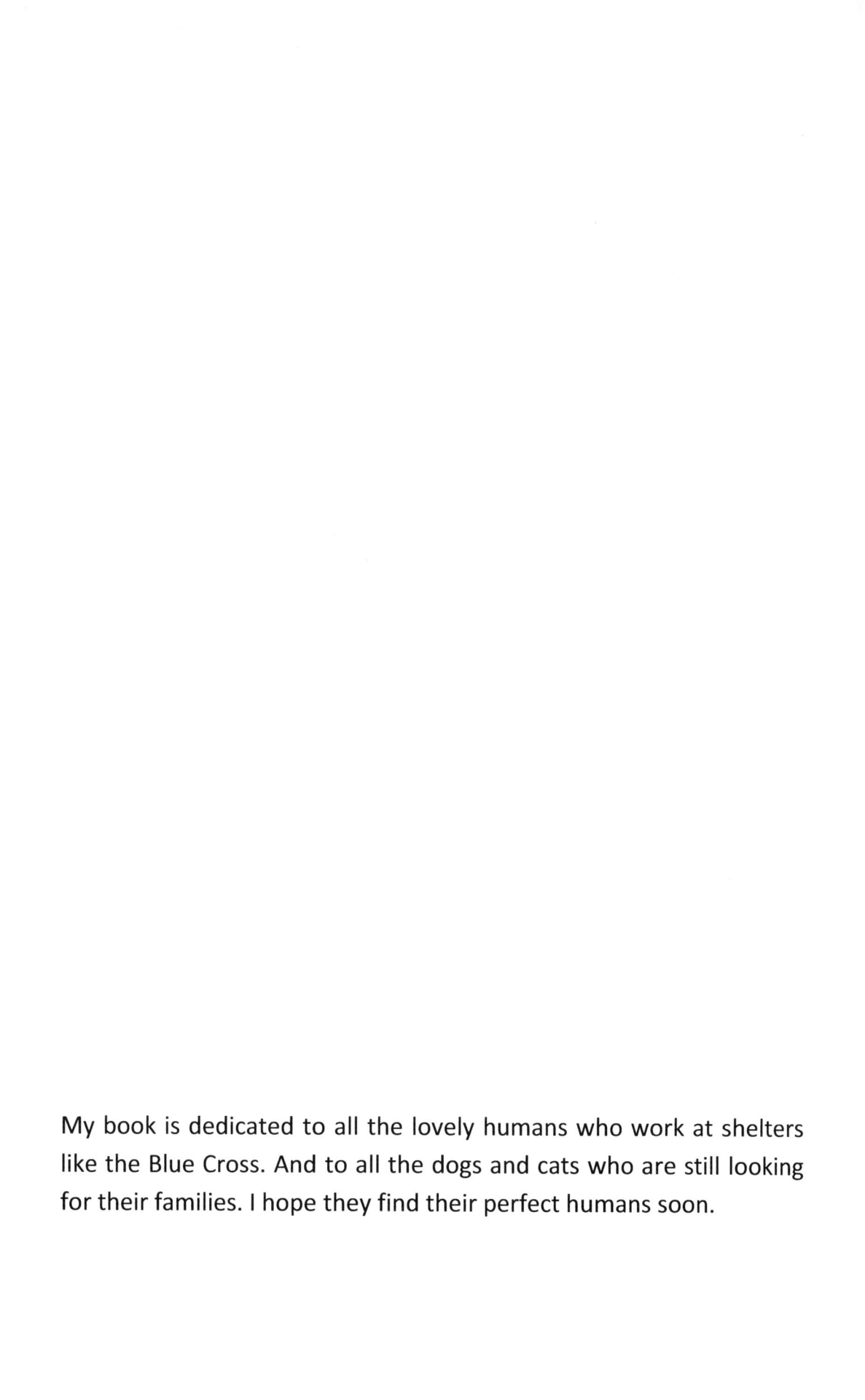

My book is dedicated to all the lovely humans who work at shelters like the Blue Cross. And to all the dogs and cats who are still looking for their families. I hope they find their perfect humans soon.

INTRODUCTION

I am Dante. Some call me Dante the Magnificent. Some call me Dante the Menace. Some call me Dante the Wonderpup. I am all these things. Well, I am two of them.

This is my book. As long as I can remember I have wanted to be a famous author. Not many dogs become authors but then not many dogs are me.

CONTENTS

1. My early life — 1
2. Who is Salmo? — 3
3. Another visitor — 6
4. Paperwork — 8
5. My family — 10
6. Home — 12
7. Learning — 14
8. Christmas — 16
9. Presents — 18
10. Birthday — 20
11. Holidays — 24
12. Summer — 26
13. Wedding — 28
14. Bonfire night — 30
15. The meaning of life — 34

CHAPTER1

MY EARLY LIFE

I was born...somewhere. I don't really know where. I don't remember my furmum or my brothers and sisters. As most dogs have lots of brothers and sisters, I suppose I must have been part of a litter, but I really don't remember them. Don't feel sad for me. You see, I have a lovely family now. And that's what matters.

I was what is called a "stray". That means a pup without a home. Stray doggies have no collar and no microchip. I was wondering around the streets of a place called Weston-Super-Mare when someone found me and put me in the back of a van.

Scary!

But don't worry, he was a friendly human and told me he was taking me somewhere nice.

And he did. He drove me all the way to a place called Hedge End, a long, long way from where I had been living, scavenging on the streets. If you're a scavenger you don't have your own bowl, and you need to find food wherever you can, mostly by looking in bins. It's horrible and I knew I deserved better. We arrived at a beautiful place called The Blue Cross, full of friendly humans and loads of dogs and cats and other lovely animals.

One human took special care of me. She promised me I wouldn't have to be a scavenger anymore. She promised me they would help me to find a family. And she promised me my own collar and a microchip.

My new home was very nice and there were loads of friends – animals and humans – to keep me company. It wasn't quite what I wanted but it was a start...

What *did* I want? Well, I dreamed of finding my own perfect family. I dreamed of having my own soft bed and perhaps a garden and nice things to eat. I dreamed of having my own collar. Maybe different collars for different occasions. I dreamed of having a microchip, even though I didn't really know what that meant. It's just that the people at the Blue Cross spoke about microchips in a way that made them sound terribly important. I dreamed of having toys and treats and fun. You know, the sort of life a great canine author deserves.

CHAPTER 2

WHO IS SALMO?

I was snoozing in my kennel one morning when the friendly human came in to see me. She put a harness on me, and a lead. This happened most mornings when the friendly girl and I went out for a walk. But this time it was different.

"Salmo," she said, "there are some people here who want to meet you. Now you be on your best behaviour for them!"

Salmo? Salmo! Who on earth was she talking to? Who is Salmo?

She kept chatting as we walked to the the place where the people waited to meet doggies. She kept saying, "You be a good boy, Salmo,"

I was a little bit miffed, it must be said. I have no idea why she thought my name was Salmo, but I knew it wasn't. Although, now that I think about it, I didn't really know what my name was. I only know that I knew what it wasn't.

I straightened up, my tail was up and wagging, and I trotted in as smartly as I could. Perhaps the people who had come to see me were my real family. Perhaps today was the day…

There were three humans waiting to meet me. The mum bent forward and the first thing she said was, "This is OUR dog! He's gorgeous,"

Oh my! She likes me…

And then she stroked me behind the ears. "He has velvet ears!"

The dad was smiling. "He is so handsome," he said, and I wondered what he was talking about. Oh my! He means me.

And then the boy stroked me, "I love him," he said, "I think this could be the one. You were right mum, we don't want a *little* dog," and he chuckled at the thought, "this little guy is the perfect size."

I kept on wagging my tail and smiling and looking happy and excited at meeting them. It wasn't difficult, because I was very happy and very excited.

Perhaps this was my family. Perhaps these were the humans who would take me home with them. They were all smiling and seemed to like me. We all walked outside together and I tried really hard to walk nicely even though I had no real experience of walking on the lead. I jumped around a bit, but that was mostly because I was excited.

We finished our little walk, all the humans were talking to the friendly girl, and then…oh no! They stroked me and said goodbye. I watched them walking away and the friendly girl took me back to my kennel.

I was so sure they were my family.

CHAPTER 3

ANOTHER VISITOR

A few days later the friendly girl came to the kennel and popped the harness on me. But this time she said, "Come on Salmo, there's someone to see you,"

She was still calling me Salmo, which was annoying, but the good thing was that someone wanted to visit me. Maybe this would be my new family.

"Hello boy!" said the friendly man. It was just one human standing there, not a family, but he was very friendly. He also looked very strong.

"Come on Salmo, let's go for a walk,"

Well, I liked the sound of that very much, even if he had the wrong name for me. Still. I wondered what my real name was…

The strong man and I set off, and when we got to the field he started to run and I ran too. I was so happy! I picked up a stick and carried it as I ran just to show him what a clever boy I am.

"Aah, clever boy," said the nice strong human, "a stick! You're a proper dog!"

Well, yes, of course I'm a proper dog, I thought to myself, but at least it was nice of him to notice.

"Come over here, let's take a selfie," and he sat down on the ground close to me and took a little gadget from his pocket. "Smile!" he said.

That's when I realised! He had the same smell as the lovely family! He had exactly the same smell. He must belong to the family. I suddenly felt very, very excited.

We ran around together and then back to the office where my friendly girl was waiting for us.

"That was great fun. He's lovely," said the strong running human, "We'll see him again on the weekend," and he was gone.

CHAPTER 4

PAPERWORK

I kept thinking about how the strong man had said they would see me again on the weekend. I kept wondering when the weekend would come. And then one day, it did.

My friendly girl came in with the harness. "Come on Salmo old boy, they're here to see you again. You be a good boy,"

I was struggling to walk. It was difficult to walk calmly on the lead like a good boy because I was so excited. And then I saw them. The family! My family! They were all there! They had even brought another human with them, a girl human. She made a big fuss of me. They all made a big fuss of me. And yes, I was right, they all had the same smell.

This must be the day. This must be my family – we've found each other at last.

But no. I thought they might take me home with them, straight away, but they didn't. They had to do something called "paperwork".

I don't know what paperwork is other than that it is very annoying. And once paperwork is done, there were medical matters to attend to. Again, I have no idea what medical matters are, and I don't remember anything about them, because soon after paperwork was done, medical matters happened and I went to sleep…

I woke up in a different place. Another kennel with a strange smell.

"There you go, Salmo old boy, you're done. You've had all your jabs and while you were under we did your microchip too," said the man in a white coat.

I wasn't quite awake, I felt a bit groggy, but I was sure I heard him say he'd done my microchip!

I went back to sleep with a big smile on my face.

CHAPTER 5

MY FAMILY

"Morning Salmo," said the friendly girl," let's get your harness on," she cuddled me as she clicked the harness buckle, "I'm going to miss you,"

I wondered why she was going to miss me. Perhaps she was going somewhere.

"Your family are here, they're waiting for you. Good luck mate, you're going to have an amazing life!"

What did she say? My family were here! They were going to take me home?

Oh wow! My tail has never wagged so much, and we ran out together to find my family. There they were. All of them!

"Here's all his paperwork," said my friendly girl. "He's had everything done, all his jabs, and his microchip too,"

"Excellent", said the Dad.

My dad.

"Come on my boy" said the Mum.

My mum.

"You're going to have to get used to being called Dante…"

Dante! That's my name. Of course it is.

I am Dante.

I always knew I was.

CHAPTER 6

HOME

We all walked to the car. A great big shiny red car. And I jumped into the back with the boy. *My* boy. My favourite human in the whole world. He stroked the fur on my neck all the way home and told me what a good boy I am. He said I was the best dog in the world.

It was quite a long journey to get to our house – my house – but it was worth it. And of course, I was a very good boy in the car. We arrived and everyone seemed so happy to show me around.

"This is your house, Dante. Here's your garden. And here's your bed…"

Everything I had been dreaming of was there. A lovely big garden to play in and a beautiful soft bed in the lounge. There was even another bed in the kitchen which was very thoughtful of them. Or so I thought until I discovered that that was where I was meant to sleep at night. I was a bit disappointed when I realised that my human family would go upstairs at night and sleep in big comfortable beds and I was expected to sleep in the kitchen.

I soon discovered where my food bowl was and where my water

bowl was and I also found some lovely new toys. Yes, life was good. Until night time arrived and the family went upstairs and shut the kitchen door.

I made it clear from the very beginning that I didn't think much of this arrangement. They didn't seem to get the message straight away, despite my singing all night long and scratching the paint off the kitchen door, and eating all the wooden spoons and dragging everything I could find all over the kitchen floor. But after the second night they understood. It didn't take me long to train them.

We all went out in the car and bought me two more comfortable doggy beds. One for the big bedroom where my mum and dad sleep and one for the bedroom where my Boy sleeps. This is a much better arrangement. I have not made a fuss in the night since then. In fact my mum is very proud of me and likes to tell people that I "slept through" from day three.

CHAPTER 7

LEARNING

My family and I were all getting along brilliantly. I was learning new things every day, and the more things I learnt the cleverer I got. My dad taught me how to sit and wait at a corner and then to cross the road with him only when he said the word, "Cross!" This is a very important thing to learn. And every time you do it right, you get a reward.

Every day we would go for a little walk and I was getting used to walking on the lead. Eventually it was time to let me off the lead, and I quickly got the idea. You can wander away from your humans, have a little sniff here and a little piddle there, but when they call your name, or whistle, you come running back to them. I am a good boy, so I got loads of rewards for doing this right, almost every time.

One day my mum and dad decided it was time for me to go to school. We found a dog training school near our house and off we went. I'd like to tell you it was fun and that I was the top dog in the class, but I can't. It was terrible. I just wasn't very good at any of the things I had to do and I didn't like the bossy human who was in charge.

I was relieved when I heard my mum say, "We'll need to find somewhere else, this isn't suitable for him. It's not as if he's going to Cruft's".

I don't know what Cruft's is but I'm glad I'm not going there.

My humans eventually found another dog training school and we all went along one evening. Oh this was so much better! I really loved the activities we did and I learnt so many things and the lovely human teachers were brilliant. I had so much fun there and I would look forward to going every week.

I can still do all the things I learnt there, like putting my paw on the paper and sitting in a hoop, and when we have visitors my mum and dad like me to show the visitors what I can do. They say I'm doing my party tricks. I am a good boy!

CHAPTER 8

CHRISTMAS

One evening, when the weather started to get cooler, I was out for a walk when I saw something that gave me a big fright. I made a low growl and I didn't want to walk any further.

"It's alright, Dante, nothing to be scared of," said my mum.

We walked on, but I really didn't like what I saw. There was a huge animal, not really a doggy, some other sort of animal, and it was glowing as if it was made of shining lights.

"It's just a silly old reindeer. Made of lights! You'll see lots more over the next few days," said mum, "because Christmas is coming,"

Christmas? Whatmas? What on earth is Christmas and why do crazy humans put enormous shiny animals in their gardens?

Christmas, my mum explained, is a really fun time of year when humans do all sorts of silly things. They put lights on everything, they even put lights in their gardens, and lights inside, they eat loads of yummy food and treats and best of all, they give each other presents. It's a nice way to cheer everyone up in the darkest, coldest time of the year.

And then my mum told me something that sounded so ridiculous I didn't really believe her. Until I saw it with my own eyes. At Christmas, humans put trees – yes, trees - inside their houses! Have you ever heard anything so silly?

Our tree soon made an appearance, and sure enough, there it was, a proper tree. Only it didn't smell like any tree I've ever known.

"You can sniff this tree, Dante, "said my humans, "But under no circumstances are you to piddle against it!"

These indoor trees are just for show. Not real trees and not for piddling on. Isn't that the most ridiculous thing ever? Still, if it means I get presents and loads of yummy food, I'm not going to complain. After all, I am a good boy.

CHAPTER 9

PRESENTS

Christmas arrived, eventually. For what seemed like months, more and more silly lights and shiny things kept appearing, and then the humans started to put nicely wrapped-up presents underneath the tree-that-wasn't-a-real-tree. They just left them there, and I wasn't allowed to open them. The smell coming from some of them was very tempting but I left them alone, because I am a good boy.

At last, I came downstairs one morning to find my mum already busy in the kitchen and my whole family awake! This was most unusual. We all sat down in the lounge, mum started to bring in food she called "nibbles" and dad made some sort of drink that got all my humans to laugh and be silly, and then at long last, we were allowed to open our presents.

My Boy, my favourite human in the whole world, helped me to rip off the paper, and I was overjoyed to find all my favourite things. A soft squeaky bone. Some tennis balls. Things to chew. Treats. A new tuggy.

And then, even more food appeared. The best kind of human food, the sort my dad has to carve. I like to help him when he carves, just in case anything falls on the floor and I have to tidy it up. On a normal Sundaylunch we might have one yummy roast, but on Christmas my mum goes crazy and does two, both at the same time. This makes my whole family very happy, and it makes me very happy as well. When I first came across Christmas I thought it was really stupid and scary. But now I understand what it's all about - food and presents and playing with your family – and I like it very, very much.

And I'm no longer scared of the pretend light-up reindeer in other people's gardens.

CHAPTER 10

BIRTHDAY

Everyone, whether dog or human, has a birthday. This means that every year (in human years) people remember the day you were born and you have a party and get presents and everyone makes a fuss of you. Obviously, this is a very nice thing. But if you are a stray you don't know when your real birthday is. So the next best thing is to have a birthday on the day you found your family and your family found you.

My birthday is the 19th January.

Every year on that date I get presents, so it's a bit like Christmas really, just without the stupid tree and the shiny reindeer. Also, my mum makes a special cake for me. Just for me.

Humans eat cake which isn't good for us dogs, so it is very important to have a specially made doggy cake. My mum is good at making a cake that I alone can enjoy! The first time I had a birthday party my mum made a delicious carrot cake just for me. She cut a slice for me to enjoy while the humans sat around and had a cup of tea and their own cake. It was all going well, until they had to pop out quickly and left me alone at home. If humans say they have to "pop out" it usually means they won't be gone for long and therefore it is too much of a faff to put on my harness and lead.

I was all alone at home, there was nobody there but me. I started to doze off. And then I remembered the delicious carrot cake. I went into the dining room, and there it was, in the middle of the table. It smelt so good. I knew I just had to have another slice, but how?

I couldn't reach the cake from where I stood, so I jumped up on the table. Yes, I know, that was a naughty thing to do. I am not supposed to jump on the table. But I blame my mum for making a delicious carrot cake.

I needed another slice of cake, but there was no slice, just a whole big chunk of cake. On top of the cake were some stupid things, sort of sticks which they had set fire to and then sung a song to me before I could eat my cake. I tasted one of the stupid sticks. It was disgusting. So I spat it out on the floor. I tried another and another. They were all horrible, so I spat them all out on the floor.

Now all that sat there on the plate was the carrot cake. My own delicious carrot cake. I am not proud of myself – I ate it all. Every last crumb. I was just licking up the last little scrap when I heard the front door open and I realised that my humans were back home.

"Oh Dante, what have you done!" they all said.

They saw me licking the crumbs from my nose.

"I ate my cake. It was delicious," I tried to explain to them.

"Look here! He's left all the candles! Oh Dante you are a menace," said my dad, "You're going to have a tummy ache tonight,"

He was right. I don't know how my dad knew, but he is obviously very clever. I did indeed have a tummy ache that night, and I didn't feel like any normal food until the next day. I actually felt quite sick. But it was worth it.

And here's the funny thing. I was a little bit worried that my humans would be cross with me because after all, I had walked on the table, spat candle things all over the floor and eaten all the cake, and yet they were quite proud of me. Several times I overheard them telling their human friends what a clever boy I am. I even heard my mum say, "He ate all the cake, but he spat out the candles – he obviously has good taste," and then they all laughed.

I wasn't a good boy that day. But it turns out I was a clever boy instead.

CHAPTER 11

HOLIDAYS

Ever since I found my family and they found me we have spent almost every single day together. Sometimes I have all of them at home, sometimes it's just my dad and me, or my mum and me or my Boy and me. Sometimes my aunt comes and pretends to play football with me. But almost every day there's someone in my family at home and in the mood to play with me.

You see, I've said "almost every day"? That's because, from time to time, my humans go away on a holiday. A holiday is something that requires humans to pack loads of things into a suitcase and then disappear for a few days or a few weeks. This *could* be a terrible thing, but I am a very lucky boy, because when my family go away on a holiday, I get to go away on my very own doggy holiday too.

My holiday happens when I go to visit another of my favourite humans and I get to live in her house and play with her dogs. She has two doggies, and they are my best friends. In fact, when we drive to my holiday I get so excited I stand up in the car and start to squeak! And I never, ever stand up in the car unless something fantastic is going to happen, like a favourite park or a favourite beach. Or a holiday!

Although I miss my humans when they go away I have such a brilliant time on my holiday that the days go by very quickly. And then, when they come back and come to fetch me, we are all so pleased to see one another again.

I think holidays are brilliant.

CHAPTER 12

SUMMER

Summer is the opposite of Christmas. Summer is warm and lovely and there are lots of hours of sunshine, but no stupid lights or presents. I get to go on longer walks because the humans really like being out and about in the summer.

The downside of summer is that I get very hot. I start to pant and my tongue sticks out. That's why it's important to go for walks near rivers or streams, and luckily, my clever humans know this. I have trained them well.

I spend a lot of time in my garden in the summer. There is so much for me to do! We have some chickens and I like to just lie in the shade and watch them. Sometimes I rush at the fence and pretend to chase them. They don't seem to mind.

One of my important jobs is keeping my family safe. I do this by making sure that unfriendly dogs and humans keep away from my garden. I run up and down and bark through the hedge and my arch enemies keep walking and don't bother to stop. I am very good at this.

I have a lovely huge water bowl in my garden – the humans call it a swimming pool – and it's lovely to sit in on the step to cool down or just stop for a drink. Sometimes my dad will put something smelly in the giant water bowl and when I go for a drink, he shouts "No Dante! No! I've just put the chlorine in! Daft boy…"

I'm not sure why he calls me a daft boy. If chlorine is so bad and so smelly why does he put it in?

CHAPTER 13

WEDDING

It was a nice warm day, and I was lying on the sofa having my mid-morning snooze, when my mum came in and said she needed to try something on me for size. It was sort-of a new collar.

"Oh Dante, that's perfect. You look so smart!" she said.

Then she called everyone in my family to come and have a look.

"Doesn't he look lovely? A bowtie really suits him," she said.

I had always hoped that I would have different collars for different occasions, and now I had a new bowtie. I wondered if we were going somewhere special.

"You'll be wearing that for the wedding," said my Dad.

Oh great. I was pleased I'd have a special occasion to go to, even though I had no idea what the wedding actually was.

And then they explained that the wedding was a special kind of party and it was going to happen right here at our house.

And then suddenly there were millions of people at our house making the garden look pretty. There were flowers and candles and twinkly lights everywhere and loads of people I didn't know came to visit. The funny thing is they seemed to know who I was, and almost everyone knew my name. I must be really famous!

"Hello Dante," everyone said, "Who's a good boy?"

People often say that to me. It's a really stupid question, isn't it? It's quite obvious who a good boy is. *I am a good boy.*

Anyway the wedding got going and all my family looked very smart indeed. But the smartest of all were my strong human and his girl. They looked especially wonderful and I discovered that the wedding was a special kind of party just for them.

A wedding is a brilliant kind of party and I recommend you go to one. As well as all the flowers and smart people there were balloons and lots of amazing food. There was even a hog roast, which is a bit like an enormous, gigantic Sundaylunch.

When it got dark all the humans stayed at my house. They didn't want to leave, and who could blame them? They were all having a lovely time, laughing and dancing and eating. I was exhausted and went to bed, even though the party carried on until the next day.

Everyone had fun. Everyone looked smart. And everyone said I looked adorable in my bowtie and I was such a good boy all day.

Weddings are not just any old kind of party. Weddings are the best kind of party.

CHAPTER 14

BONFIRE NIGHT

It was a cold dark night and I was curled up on my sofa enjoying a snooze. My mum and dad were sitting on their sofa and they were watching television. I quite like television when there is a good programme on it. I really like programmes about other dogs. In fact I like programmes about all sorts of animals. Mum says my favourites are called David Attenborough. Whenever there's a David Attenborough on I like to sit quietly and look at the wonderful scenes.

This particular night I was just snoozing because there were no David Attenboroughs on and whatever the humans were watching was SO boring. Suddenly a loud noise woke me up. It was deafening and it made me jump. My dad pulled the curtain back a little bit, and there in the dark night sky we saw some bright lights.

"Damn fireworks," said Dad,

"They start earlier and earlier every year," said Mum.

I was puzzled. What were these noises and lights that start earlier and earlier?

My humans explained it all to me. There's this thing called Bonfire Night. Most humans find it very entertaining but for dogs and chickens and cats and other fur and feather friends too, I think, it's a terrible, stupid time. Humans let off fireworks. These make very pretty patterns in the sky but they also make loud bangs and whooshing noises which frighten us.

The best thing to do on Bonfire Night – and the nights before and after, because it seems like some humans don't know what day it is – is to read my guide to staying safe on Bonfire Night. Here it is.

Dante's Guide to Staying Safe on Bonfire Night – advice to puppies

1. Stay close to your humans at all times. Very close. They will protect you.
2. Go outside for a wee before the noises start (your humans will advise you on this) and then stay put inside until they finish.
3. Cuddle up on the sofa with a human and put your paw on their leg. This will help to reassure them if they are scared.
4. If the noises get too much there are safe places around the house, like under your dad's desk where you can sit on his feet, or under the big bed.
5. Ask your humans to get a special collar for you which will help you to relax. It seems to work for me.

6. Remember you are safe indoors with your favourite people while outsider there are loads of stupid humans standing around in the dark and the wet and the cold and the mud, pretending to have fun. You can snooze on your warm sofa until it's all over.

   And they think dogs are stupid!

CHAPTER 15

THE MEANING OF LIFE

I was lying on one of my favourite sofas. The one which lets me see what's going on in the garden as well as who comes in through the door. The sun was coming in through the window, making the fur on my back feel lovely and warm. I was half awake and half asleep. I wasn't really dreaming, just thinking.

I was thinking about the meaning of life.

When I was a stray doggy, wandering around the streets and living the life of a scavenger, I wished for all sorts of things. I wished for a collar. Several collars, for different occasions. I wished for my own water bowl and a food bowl all my own. I longed for toys and treats.

But what I wanted most of all was some humans to share these things with me. I realise now that having loads of different collars for different occasions is nice, but the nicest thing in the whole world is to have humans to love. And I, Dante the Magnificent, famous canine author, have the best humans in the whole world. They are my family and I love them.

Now my wish is for all the stray doggies out there, all the scavengers who don't have a microchip, to find their families, and to live a life like mine.

If you are a human reading this, do yourself a favour. Find a dog. Your dog. There are lots of doggies waiting for humans to love – one of them is waiting for you.

ABOUT THE AUTHOR AND HIS HELPERS

Dante Miles lives in Hampshire where he is a full-time family pet and aspirant author.
His hobbies include chasing a squeaky ball, playing tuggy with a rope, paddling in streams, running around in the woods, getting muddy, watching wildlife documentaries and snoozing.

Edyth Miles also lives in Hampshire and spends part of her day at a large comprehensive secondary school with lots of lovely teenagers, and the rest of her day with her crazy family. She is Dante's human mum and slave.

Hattie Hyder lives in the Surrey Hills and is an award winning illustrator, but she doesn't like to talk about that, she'd rather get on with drawing. Her preferred tools are a scratchy old pen nib and a very messy box of watercolours.

Printed in Great Britain
by Amazon